DESIGN

and decorate

COLOUR SCHEMES

NEW
HOLLAND

Lesley Taylor

To Abigail, my daughter, with thanks for all the hours she waited to get on the computer, whilst I was writing the book.

First published in 1997 by
New Holland Publishers (UK) Ltd
London • Cape Town • Sydney •Auckland

24 Nutford Place
London W1H 6DQ
United Kingdom

80 McKenzie Street
Cape Town 8001
South Africa

3/2 Aquatic Drive
Frenchs Forest, NSW 2086
Australia

Unit 1A
218 Lake Road
Northcote
Auckland
New Zealand

10 9 8 7 6 5 4 3 2

ISBN 1 85368 941 6

Managing Editor: Coral Walker
Special photography: Janine Hosegood
Designed by: Grahame Dudley Associates
Editor: Emma Callery
Illustrator: Madelaine Floyd

Reproduction by Modern Age Repro House Ltd, Hong Kong
Printed and bound in Singapore by Tien Wah Press (Pte) Ltd

Contents

Style *file* 24

Introduction

Welcome to **Colour Schemes**, the book designed to give you practical help when designing and decorating your home. Each chapter addresses the topics you need to be familiar with to design a room successfully. It first explains the difference between tone and colour, and considers their individual characteristics and how they effect the look of a room. This is then followed by a description of how colour works and, most importantly, how to successfully use contrasting colours in the same room. On pages 18-23, I show you how to combine colours and patterns to create a certain style of room, giving tips on the simplest forms of colour scheme and explain why they work.

If you are planning your room from scratch, then you may be confused by the many different room styles now available: Mediterranean to country cottage, town house to contemporary. To help you overcome the difficult decisions, this book has a specially designed section called Style File, showing in detail the various decorative styles available for most rooms in the home.

Whatever aspect of colour scheming interest you, it is undoubtedly covered in the book. So whether you want to learn about colour theory or just become familiar with the elements that create a Tuscan dining room or feminine bedroom, it is all covered in simple to understand terms within these pages.

Happy designing.

Lesley Taylor.

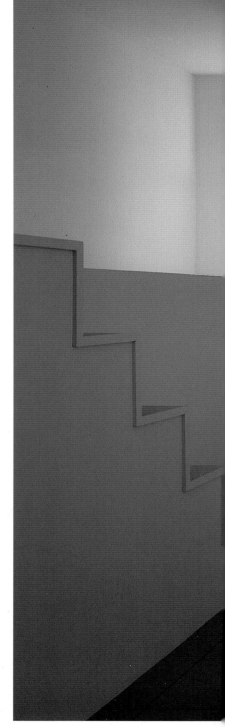

Dynamics
of colour

DIFFERENT MOODS

The same space can be given very different looks with skilful use of colour. Shades of blue maximize space; red creates warmth and intimacy; acid yellow adds life and vibrancy; clean, crisp greens and blues create a fresh look; contrasting blue and pink make perfect companions; cool blue meets restful green, creating calm.

Colour is undoubtedly the most important tool available to anyone decorating their home as it can add life and vitality to an uninspiring room. It also has the power to produce a variety of moods and an atmosphere that can affect the very quality of life lived by its occupants. You can use colour to make a small room look larger and more spacious, or to make a large room smaller and more intimate. By the subtle use of colour alone you can warm up a north-facing room or cool down the sunniest of walls.

We live in a colourful world, so why are so many of us hesitant when it comes to applying colour in our own homes? Possibly it is because we have only recently entered an age where technological advances enable us to produce paints, fabrics and wall coverings in practically any desired shade. This is such a contrast to the old safe approach to decorating chosen by our parents, that I am sure we merely require time to adjust.

Colour requires both confidence and caution. It is the easiest, cheapest way to transform a room – and the most daring. Which is why, if we are to use it successfully, we must learn how colour works, harness its

powers and use it in an educated manner. Once you understand colour, you then have the ability to transform your surroundings, creating an atmosphere unique to you.

Importance

of tone

While colour is very powerful and adds atmosphere to a room, it is the way in which we use tone that affects the actual shape of the finished room.

The word tone describes the lightness or darkness of a colour, and this is altered by the addition of black or white. I find the easiest way to translate colour into tone is to imagine the room or item you are considering as it would be seen in a black and white photograph. If it was all of the same tonal value, the picture would appear completely flat. It is only the variation of tone that adds depth to the photograph.

SPACE ENHANCING
▶ These diagrams show how tone can be used to improve the proportions of a room or disguise problem areas.

SUCCESSFUL SCHEMES
▼ This well-planned, neutral scheme shows just how important tone is when planning a colour scheme.

To make a room feel larger, decorate in light colours as light is then reflected.

To bring the walls in and ceiling down, use warm colours.

Dark and warm colours advance. A wall painted in a dark colour is drawn in.

Cool colours recede. A wall painted in a cool colour appears further away.

A dark floor covering makes the floor seem smaller and draws the eye downwards.

To lower a ceiling use a colour which is slightly darker than the walls.

To raise a ceiling use a colour which is lighter than the walls.

To lower a ceiling in a large room paint the top section of the walls to match.

To widen a corridor use a very light colour on the walls, ceiling and floor.

To shorten a corridor, paint the end wall in a dark or warm colour.

To alter the proportions of a corridor, decorate the ceiling and floor in a darker colour.

As a general guide, dark colours advance and pale colours recede as they reflect more light, making a room appear larger. This is why so many modern properties have their rooms, and ceilings in particular, painted white: to create the illusion of space and height.

Tone can be used to great effect in a narrow hallway or corridor. By applying a darker tone to the ceiling than the walls (and in some case on properties with very tall ceilings, by bringing the same tone down to the picture rail), you considerably reduce the appearance of the ceiling height. By adding a floor covering which is also of a deeper tone than the walls, you create the effect of pushing back the walls, making the corridor appear wider.

Another common problem in modern properties is the long sitting room with its windows at one or either end on the narrow walls. By applying the theory of dark colours advancing, a substantial pair of curtains in a tone deeper than the walls can successfully draw in the window walls. In this way, the proportions of the room are visually adjusted, making it appear squarer (see the illustration on page 9 for other ways to improve on the proportions of your rooms).

Many people enjoy the calm simplicity of a monochromatic colour scheme; a room decorated only in tones of one colour. The room opposite, for example, is decorated in a variety of blues such as lavender blue and green blue. But, in addition, there are varying strengths of tone included, creating a finished

room of great visual interest. Imagine this room with the door coloured the same tone as the walls, and with the white woodwork and picture frame painted in a green blue. If this were the case, the room would have much less impact and would look very flat and uninteresting.

TONALITY

The calm simplicity of this scheme comes from the consideration of colour and tone. By varying the shades of blue, greater interest is given to the room.

How colour
works

Colour is so powerful that it can transform the quality of a room in terms of mood and proportion, so a knowledge of colour theory is invaluable to the home decorator and designer. By understanding the colour wheel, for example, choosing an accent to pep up a bland room becomes a far simpler exercise.

The wheel is broken up into three basic colour types: primary, secondary, and tertiary (or intermediate) colours. Primary colours are the only ones that cannot be made by the mixing of other colours and create the foundation of all theory. They are red, yellow and blue (at 11 o'clock, 3 o'clock and 7 o'clock on the photograph opposite).

Secondary colours are derived from mixing together equal amounts of two primary colours. For example, yellow mixed with red will give you orange (1 o'clock, opposite), blue and yellow creates green (5 o'clock), and blue and red produces violet (9 o'clock). These are known as the secondary colours. Tertiary or intermediate colours fall between the secondary hues and supply us with many different shades.

Now that you are familiar with the colour wheel you can begin to understand some of the other categories. Harmonious colours all have the same base, for example, blue, as in green-blue, violet-blue and violet. They are found next to each other on the colour wheel. These colours always combine well and when used together create a scheme that is easy on the eye.

Contrasting colours are those that lie opposite each other on the wheel, the strongest of which are direct opposites, such as

THE COLOUR WHEEL
The colours in the colour wheel are always found in the same position because each colour, whether it is secondary, intermediate, or shades between, are always achieved by mixing the same proportions of the original colours.

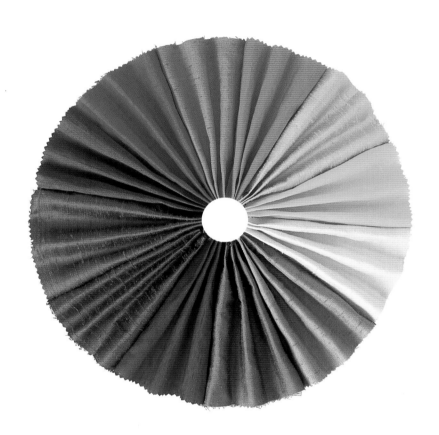

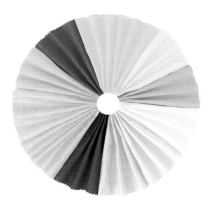

PRIMARY COLOURS

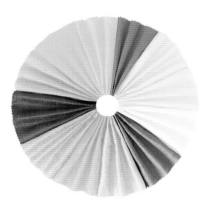

SECONDARY COLOURS

green and orange or lavender and yellow. If you are decorat-ing a room with two contrasting colours, be cautious, and always make sure that one dominates or you could have a scheme that is uneasy on the eye, as they tend to compete.

The colours in the wheel can also fall into two further categories: warm and cool. Warm colours are found on the top of the wheel; choose these if you want a cosy and welcoming colour scheme. Warm colours draw in a room and they include reds, yellows, pinks and oranges. Cool colours, however, tend to have a calming effect on a room, making it look more spacious and formal. These colours are found on the opposite side of the wheel and include violets, blues and greens.

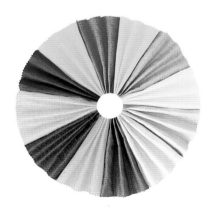

TERTIARY COLOURS

Accent and
contrast colours

**CHOOSING
ACCENT
COLOURS**
Accents can be
taken from any part
of the colour wheel,
depending on the
main colour in your
decorating scheme. It
is only a matter of
personal choice and
what effect you want to
achieve. The most
striking accents are
those from the
opposite side of the
wheel to the main
colour scheme.

Have you ever experienced that disheartening feeling when you have spent weeks planning your new room? You have deliberated, pondered and agonized over the patterns, shades and the important tones of your room, only to stand back and view your finished room in the knowledge that 'there is something definitely missing'. Well, the possibility is that if the room has been well planned and is made up of one or two well-balanced colours it will benefit from the use of an accent colour – a different, contrasting colour – to give relief and dimension to your room.

Accents don't have to come in the form of a fabric, paint or wall covering. In fact, these would quite often offer too large a block of colour. Instead, the occasional lamp, picture or even well-placed blanket or throw can be the perfect solution.

Accents should always be used with restraint, less is more is definitely the right approach. Use them in patches and don't dot them around. If you use a tonal variation of the colour that predominates in your colour scheme, it will no longer act as an accent. Instead, it will become part of the main colour scheme, making the room too busy. One carefully chosen cushion in your accent colour will have more of an impact on your room than four of the same all positioned like soldiers on your sofa.

The bedroom featured here is the perfect example of a well-used accent. The room is made up of equal portions of the blue and cream checked fabric and the plain wall panelling. The colours are soft, and while there is an interesting mix of plaid and check, the red accent is needed to pep up the scheme. The red in this case is a contrast accent because it is a colour found on the opposite side of the colour wheel to the blue of the main scheme. A number of other accent colours could have been used in this room, such as pink and pale yellow, but the red offers the most impact precisely because it is such a contrast.

COUNTRY CHECKS
The red picture and blankets act as a very successful accent in this room, contrasting with the predominant blue of the check bedding and curtains.

**BRIGHT
YELLOW**
A hallway painted in bright yellow and white is given a contrasting accent with the addition of the black vase.

Contrast accents are perfect for adding definition to a mono-chromatic scheme where shades and tones are all of one colour. A room decorated in different shades of peach, for example, will always look good with the addition of a green accent (again, shades that are not close together on the colour wheel). This can be in the form of plants grouped in the corner of the room together with a small green footstool placed on the opposite side for balance. Likewise, a soft blue (a cool colour) bedroom can benefit from the warmth introduced by a small touch of pink, such as a bowl of flowers, or a soft pink blanket folded at the foot of the bed.

As you become familiar with the effects of a coloured accent on a room you will soon begin to recognize examples of this technique when you look through your favourite interiors magazines. You will also notice rooms that would benefit from the addition of an accent here and there. But be tactful, not everyone will take kindly to you offering them the benefit of your newly found knowledge.

ACCENTS ADD INTEREST

▼ This yellow nursery, furnished principally in white, is offset by a few accents of blue. Imagine the room without the accent; it would be rather uninteresting.

Colour and
fabric design

Many of us may find we need to decorate a room around an existing patterned sofa, or we might fall in love with a range of bedding and need to design a room around that. If you are in that situation, you can quite often benefit from the expertise of the person who designed that particular bedding or the fabric covering the sofa.

The designer will have spent a great deal of time trying different colours and shades together in their fabric, until the right effect had been achieved. If you are planning to have this fabric in your home it means that you find the same blend of colours

SWEET DREAMS
Designing around a patterned fabric can be simpler than you think as long as you take note of the proportions in which the designer has used the colours. In this instance, blue is followed by white and then yellow and pink in smaller quantities.

are also to your taste. So take advantage of it.

First look closely at the fabric and consider the proportions in which the colours have been used. Then make a note of them, the greatest first. Take the fabric on the bed featured here, for example. The background colour, blue, is the predominant colour in the design, followed by the white, and then the yellow and pink in almost equal quantities.

Now consider your room. What element will take the largest block of colour? In the case of this bedroom, it was the walls, followed by the impressive ceiling, and then the floor. Always remember to think of the room when it is full of furniture; the floor area may equal the ceiling area when the room is empty, but this changes with the addition of the bed. Make a note of this information, and decorate the room with colour in the same proportions as used in the fabric.

So, to complement this fabric, the room has been decorated with the main block of blue on the walls, the white on the ceiling (the next largest area), and then the pink and yellow in smaller quantities. Mellow yellow tones were introduced in the wood on the floor, and in splashes of a purer yellow on the bed valance and as a border. Finally, the pink was used as an all-important accent on the cushion on the chair and, to add balance, the pink carnation in the vase on the side table.

CLEVER TEXTILES
◀ Fabric designers spend a lot of time working out a good balance of colour. So when a large expanse of fabric dominates, such as a bedcover or sofa, you can be guided by this to decorate the rest of the room.

Colour as a
backdrop

**COLOURS THAT
COMPLEMENT
EACH OTHER**
The peaches and
blues used to
decorate the room
opposite work well
together because they
are complementary
colours on the wheel.

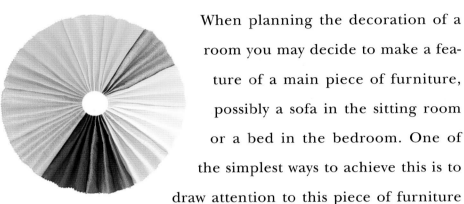

When planning the decoration of a room you may decide to make a feature of a main piece of furniture, possibly a sofa in the sitting room or a bed in the bedroom. One of the simplest ways to achieve this is to draw attention to this piece of furniture by using patterned fabric on or around it. This can be further enhanced by keeping the remainder of the room as simple as possible by decorating it in blocks of varying tones of one colour: giving the central feature a monochromatic backdrop.

Here your knowledge of colour theory comes to the fore. Most patterned fabrics are made up of a number of different colours, giving you various options when choosing the background colour. If the fabric incorporates blues, peaches and yellows, for example, a large room may benefit from being decorated in tones of peach, as this is a warm colour and therefore advances, making the room cosier. A north-facing room could be made brighter by introducing a mellow yellow wooden floor and sunny yellow walls, or a smart sitting room would take on a formal air with the use of cool blues. At the same time, don't forget to take advantage of the power of tone to reduce the ceiling height, for example, or improve the proportions of an awkwardly shaped room (see page 9).

Rooms featuring soft furnishings with plenty of patterns on them are best served in this way. The bed opposite, for example,

A COSY CHILD'S ROOM

Warm tones of peach used simply and plainly in the background make the heavily patterned bed a central feature in this cosy bedroom.

has been set in a simply decorated room featuring a warm shade of peach on the plainly constructed tongue and groove wall. The carpet, too, is a suitably neutral tone. Such simplicity only serves to throw the bed with its patterned quilt cover into relief, turning it into the focal point of the room. An equally success-fully decorated bedroom using this idea is featured on page 52.

Coordinated
colour schemes

A coordinated colour scheme is one in which various products are linked together by a common motif or design and the same range of colours. Many interior design houses put together ranges of coordinating fabrics, wallpapers and borders. These are specifically designed to appeal to the home decorator who either feels most comfortable with a theme that runs through all the items in a room or for those lacking the confidence to choose their own combinations. This is not to say that the professional designer doesn't use such ranges. On the contrary, you will find interior design studios full of such collections. But the majority of designers will usually only use one or two items from a range, preferring to create a more individual look by incorporating products from different suppliers. Different patterns can be carefully combined as long as they are based on the same colours.

If the feel of a range appeals to you, but you want to ensure a more individual room, look at alternative wall coverings, for example, but continue to use the fabrics and borders that are suggested in the main collection. There is one thing to note, however, and that is it is normally the border that accentuates a coordinated scheme. Sometimes just omitting the border or changing it for something a little different makes a room look more designed, and less off-the-shelf.

CLEVER COORDINATING
▶ This cleverly designed coordinated range is linked together both by colour and by design. You can see elements from the design of both the fabrics and the border incorporated into the material used on the roller blind.

MAKING COLOUR WORK FOR YOU
◀ Refer to your colour wheel whenever you are coordinating different elements. It will help you develop your ideas.

STYLE *file*

COUNTRY CREAM AND PINK
▲ Motifs from this stylized wallpaper decorate the kitchen units and walls to give the room a very person-alized, and at the same time unified, feel. This is further enhanced by the use of cream and pink on the walls and in the soft furnishings.

A SPLASH OF COLOUR
▶ This stunning vase of flowers gives the room a lift because the predom-inant use of red contrasts so strongly with the blue wall behind. The small amount of white and pink in the arrangement supplies contrast.

By now you will be familiar with the way colour and tone can affect a room, and I am sure you can handle accents and monochromatic schemes with ease. These are all the basis of good design practice, but to be able to turn your hand to confident interior design you need to be familiar with the various styles of decor.

The style of curtain you choose, and the shape and colour of your sofa all have an effect on the look of your finished room. A feather-filled chintz sofa would look completely out of place in a Mediterranean style living room, for example. In the same way, a hand-painted terracotta pot would have no place sitting in a Georgian dining room.

Learning what styles of furniture and furnishings work together to create a certain look is very important and one of the simplest ways of doing this is by flipping through magazines and breaking down the rooms into elements such as style of cur-tains, fabrics used, design of wallpapers, and the finish of the fireplaces. You will soon find that you identify the items that set the tone of the room, and those that enhance it.

In Style File, we feature the most important rooms in the house, each decorated in a different colourway and style, and discuss how the colours and elements are best put together.

TOP LEFT
The traditional Georgian red is given a contemporary twist with the sponged panels and hand-painted fish.

TOP RIGHT
Muted colours, a plaid fabric and wood combine in an easy simplicity. The ties on the bedding add to this homespun feel.

BOTTOM LEFT
Cornflower blue and soft green contrast with sunshine yellow, pink and orange in this surprisingly coordinated sitting room.

BOTTOM RIGHT
The old and the new are unified by timeless yellow paint on the walls and traditional fabric over the chair seats.

Living rooms

Regardless of the form of decoration chosen for your living room, it will undoubtedly fall into one of two categories: an informal room for relaxing and entertaining in, or a room that is used only occasionally; one from which the chaos of normal, everyday life is excluded. So before you begin, write a brief defining the functions of the room. If the room is for entertaining, for example, you will require several tables on which to put drinks and the occasional nibble. A family space, on the other hand, may need to house the television, music systems or even a computer.

As with most rooms, it is best to invest in the most important pieces of furniture. A good quality sofa will last for years, and with re-upholstery and throws, it can take on a variety of looks.

FLORAL ACCENTS
▶ This yellow and gold room will lift the spirits of both family and friends. The patterns on the footstool and blinds act as the perfect accent to the main yellow scheme.

CALM, COOL BLUE
◀ This monochromatic living room is the ideal place in which to relax, as shades of blue are calming and soothing after a day's strenuous activities.

Daffodil yellow
and grass green

Harmonious colours such as yellow and green are easy on the eye because they lie next to each other on the colour wheel. They work together particularly well here as the fresh shade of green used to colourwash the walls is tonally much nearer to yellow than, say, a shade of sage green would be.

The walls have been split using a dado rail which helps to lower the high ceiling. The proportions of the room are such that it could appear rather grand, and while a swag pelmet has been chosen, it is in an informal style using a soft fabric. The under curtain made from a fine sheer fabric diffuses and softens the light which could otherwise be a little harsh through such a large window. The wooden floor which has been stripped and varnished, brings a rustic quality to the room, once again enhancing this casual atmosphere.

A pair of lamps have been positioned on either side of the fireplace, highlighting the recesses when illuminated. This switches the focal point of the room from the window in the daytime to the chimney breast in the evening.

A group of patterned cushions adds a splash of additional colour and also softens the squareness of the sofa. The carefully grouped pictures above the sofa enable the owner to bring some of his or her personality

MELLOW YELLOW
▶ This well-proportioned room has been decorated to produce a fresh and comfortable living space. The pale shades of green and yellow are cool and relaxing to live with.

PRIMARY AND SECONDARY COLOURS
◀ Green is a secondary colour derived from yellow (mixed with blue) and therefore together they work in harmony.

in penthouse chic

into the room. In addition, they have been arranged so that none of the pictures is above the height of the overmantel mirror. In this way the height of the room is visually lowered as the eye-line is kept to a reasonable level.

ACCESSORIES
▲ Choose the colours of your accessories according to which shade you prefer to highlight in your colour scheme.

Coffee and cream
a classic look

The group of colours known as neutrals range from brown and creams through to whites, and when it comes to colour trends, these colours reappear on a regular basis, mainly because they are so easy to live with.

Neutrals have been teamed here with soft peaches and terracotta, and the finished effect is a classic and warm room. The plain cream sofa and chair in the foreground keep the room light and fresh, while the rug adds contrast.

NEUTRALITY
▶ Coffee and cream work well together because they are neutral shades that tone harmoniously. All the colours in this room have been chosen from one particular area of the colour wheel. An arrangement of bright flowers in the fireplace would bring a totally new dimension to the room.

MONO- CHROME INTERIORS

▲ Plan the colours of your room by pooling different shades and see how they work together side by side.

The walls in both the main sitting area and the conservatory beyond have been split using a dado rail. The main room also has a picture rail that breaks up the wall yet again and keeps the eye level to a reasonable height. The designer could have also drawn down the ceiling height by using a colour on the frieze and ceiling that was deeper in tone than the walls. But in this case it would have made the room too oppressive.

Details like dado and picture rails have been in vogue recently and while this trend continues they will look as good in modern properties as in period houses. However, once this becomes less fashionable, the decor in modern properties will soon date if these features remain. They can be decorated either to blend in with the background colour or make useful areas of varying colour should you wish to use them in this way.

One of the most noticeable points that sets this room apart from neutral rooms of the past, is the style of furniture and accessories. The sofa and chair are a timeless classic style, but the dining table is an up-to-the-minute wrought-iron design, as are all the contemporary *objets d'art* on the shelves and fireplace. The careful choice of colour unites the disparate styles.

SHADES OF BROWN

▶ The ultimate in natural colour – roasted coffee beans display a range of dark browns in many different tones.

Create a relaxing mood
with warm blues

A smooth, glowing, beautifully finished wooden floor acts as the perfect background in the comfortable family room featured opposite. Large, undressed windows and plain walls make the room appear as airy and spacious as possible, while a mixture of blue furniture and soft furnishings create a relaxed atmosphere.

Blue is known for its calming properties, but also has the reputation of appearing cold. However, when lavender blue tones (moving towards the red, warmer side of the colour wheel) are introduced and teamed up with the warmth of a mellow wooden floor, such as the one featured in this photograph, a far more inviting blue room is created.

Great attention to detail has been paid here with the careful mixing of patterned fabrics used for cushions and a throw on the sofa. The simplest and most foolproof form of pattern mixing is to layer the design, varying the scale and density. For example, a large pattern with a dense background teams well

with a smaller scale flowing pattern with a more open background. Both of these also work successfully in a scheme incorporating geometric checks and stripes of various sizes. Always try to keep the fabrics within the same range of shade – here they are all shades of blue, for example. Or, if you have many

STENCILS
▲ A simple stencilled design in a soft lavender blue applied to the dresser in the large living space opposite softens the appearance of the piece of furniture and adds interest, too.

PATTERN MIXING
◀ When selecting your fabrics it is worth grouping the swatches so that you can really get a feel for the way they work together.

different colours or tones of colour in a room, look for a multi-coloured piece of fabric that will unite them all.

To redress the balance away from an overwhelming sense of blue, warm coral pink accent colours have been chosen for flowers on the side table and featured in the picture on the far wall. These details may not be very obvious at first sight but they are very important to the overall finished scheme.

LIGHT AND AIRY
Light blue and peach are the perfect colours for maintaining the airy feel of this room and at the same time add warmth to the space.

Kitchens

The kitchen of years ago, with its real fire, was always the heart of the home, an area in which the family gathered, women gossiped and the men warmed themselves after a long day's work. Then, with the introduction of central heating and labour-saving devices, this all changed, and the kitchen became a practical workspace. The family kitchen is now experiencing a revival, however, and it is being used as a place to eat, work and entertain.

When choosing the colours for your kitchen, don't forget that it is one of the first rooms in which you spend time each morning. So the colours used should be restful and look as good in daylight as in the evening when you entertain. Also remember that colour is supplied by china and utensils and these will have a great impact on the balance of a room.

ACCENTUATING THE POSITIVE
▼ The layout of these Mediterranean blue units makes the most of the space available in this galley kitchen. They also contrast beautifully with the wooden work surfaces and warm terracotta walls.

COUNTRY STYLE

▼ Painted wood in cream, and patterned accents in blue, combine to make a sophisticated country kitchen.

COOL WHITE

◄ In this largely white kitchen, the accent of blue above the cooker is all that was needed to bring it to life.

Deep red and dark oak
for a rich

COLOUR VARIATION

Initially, it is the deep burgundy red that greets the eye in this room, but the blue vase and fruit bowl in the foreground go a long way towards alleviating what might otherwise be an unremitting heaviness.

The units in this characterful kitchen are a basic dark oak, but it is the bold decoration that gives the room its atmosphere. The dark crimson balances well with the wood, and while it could have appeared quite heavy, the decorator has chosen a gloss finish for the painted walls, taking advantage of its reflective qualities. Both windows are undressed to allow for maximum light, and the ledges on the lower sash windows supply an

b a c k g r o u n d

additional display area for the owner's beloved collection of china dogs.

A paper border brings relief from the plain walls and introduces pattern to the room. This links with the fabric on the carved oak chair, while a larger scale pattern on the kelim rug decorates the floor. An old plate rack adds needed extra storage and, grouped together with old wooden trays, it supplies a further interesting feature.

This kitchen is very homely and looks as if it has evolved over the years. The secret to this form of decorating is to keep to historical colours, use a blend of older wooden chairs and cupboards, and display your favourite collection of china and books. Historical colours are often used by designers to create archive-style fabrics and wall coverings. There is currently a revival in historical type paints such as distemper and casein and many manufacturers are now producing collections that include traditional colours from various times in history such as Georgian and Victorian. These are perfect for use in traditionally decorated rooms such as this kitchen.

The electrical points in this room have been painted to blend with the walls (blocks of white in a colour scheme like this would look very obvious indeed). As an alternative to painting points, it is also possible to buy coloured or even transparent ones.

FRUITFUL INTERIORS

It is not only the colour of a ceramic bowl that enhances a colour scheme, but the fruit that is in it, too. A judicious choice of contents can bring a strong accent to your kitchen.

THE FINER POINTS

◄ Old wooden pieces of furniture and carved animals add a rustic charm to this room.

Soft blue provides
contemporary colour

CHECK IT OUT
▶ Checks and plaids will always add character to a room and are the perfect way to introduce tonal variation or an accent or two.

COLOURFUL CROCKERY
▼ Specially purchased kitchenware should be seen, and not hidden away. With so many well-designed pieces now available at affordable prices, why not display them for all to see?

A kitchen like this one is very versatile. Depending on the colour in which it is painted and the surrounding decor, it can take on a variety of different looks. Here, shades of soft blue and terracotta have been carefully combined to create a simple and contemporary atmosphere.

The pale blue gives the room a calm, uncluttered air, and as it is teamed with an off-white, it is also deliciously soft. The floor is covered with linoleum in a practical, pale terracotta shade that is linked to the rest of the kichen with its blue inserts. The colour of these is deeper than the units, supplying a variation of tone, and therefore a dimension to the decor. The colour of the floor is then lifted into the main scheme via the introduction of a terracotta bowl and a picture framed in natural wood. Earth colours like these blend especially well with Mediterranean shades of blue, pink and white.

The gingham Roman blind over the French windows adds a splash of colour to the kitchen, too: checks and plaids have a wonderful traditional quality. The simplicity of the blind combined with the freshness of the gingham means that colour is injected but without detracting from the airy quality of this kitchen. By using the gingham elsewhere, such as in napkins or chair seats, for example, the fabric could also be used to add further tonal variation in the room.

While the walls and the kitchen units are painted the same

colour, important tonal variations are supplied by the blue glass-ware. The incidental basket of lemons near the French windows adds an accent to the room, as the vibrant yellow contrasts so strongly with the essentially blue colour scheme. The room design also benefits greatly from the kitchenware. It is such a shame to hide away well designed pieces: if they have been chosen to enhance your kitchen, display them for all to see.

THE NATURAL KITCHEN

The calm serenity of this kitchen is achieved by the blending of soft blue with simple off-white. The basket of lemons and bowl of plums are a charmingly natural way of using colour accents.

Retro style uses
vivid turquoise

THE RETRO KITCHEN

This is a compact and unified kitchen relying on a strong sense of colour to knit its disparate elements together. Although the colours are taken from all around the colour wheel they work well together because the turquoise predominates and everything else is subservient to it.

This retro-style kitchen was decorated around its magnificent refrigerator that is so immediately redolent of the 1950s. The base units were painted the same colour and while, with the exception of the storage units, the kitchen is unfitted, the room has a contained feel because the turquoise is continuously used from the base unit round to the refrigerator. The strong colour is only used at a low level, with the wall cupboards and open shelving above painted white. This keeps the room as spacious as possible because the cool white reflects light, making the walls appear to recede.

Red is used as an accent colour to lift the room. Note the way

it has been applied in varying blocks, from the waste bin to the small splash of colour supplied by the taps and with the slightly larger group of red cups. If the crockery had been scattered around the area, it would not have had the same impact.

The kitchen occupies the minimum of space, but it still supplies all the facilities needed in a working kitchen: the practical cooker, the dishwasher, water supply, storage and the refrigerator. Also, the layout falls into the 'triangle principle' where all the important elements – water supply, cooking area, and fridge – are contained in a triangle.

A simple checkerboard design has been created using the black and white tiles, blending the area between the black worktop and the white units. The black continues through the units, on the handles and down to floor. In contrast, chrome kitchen utensils hang from the window frame, ensuring they are always at hand, and as chrome is very much in keeping with this retro style, the theme is continued with other kitchen accessories.

If the decorating colours had not been limited so religiously to the core colours of turquoise, red, black and white, the end result could easily have been overpowering and messy, Instead, the kitchen is both compact and stylish.

GETTING THE BALANCE
▼ Turquoise, red, white and black supplies a stylish colour scheme. But don't use the red and turquoise in equal quantities as they tend to compete since they are on opposite sides of the colour wheel.

Dining areas

These days, few people have the luxury of a separate, formal dining room used purely for entertaining, which is why there are so many multi-functional areas that fulfil more than just the need for a pleasant space in which to eat. A dining room can be a quiet backwater where the children can do their homework or books can be read in a comfy chair. Alternatively, the eating area can become a hive of activity, by being positioned in one of the main rooms, either in the kitchen, or as a part of the living room, where people cannot only dine but watch television, talk, or work at the table.

Once the function of the room has been determined, you can turn your thoughts to the design or colour scheme of the room. This should be a well-balanced mix of your own personality and a style that is sympathetic to both the age of the property and the proportions of the room.

MODERN DINING

◀ The main room and key pieces of furniture are all painted in relaxing, cool blues and pale greens.

LIVING/DINING

▲ Colourful coordinating fabrics create a relaxed atmosphere in what could otherwise be a rather formal room.

TUSCAN-STYLE

◀ A Mediterranean balcony was the inspiration for this cheerful dining room. Wooden flooring and yellow, colourwashed walls create the perfect backdrop for the dining table and its weathered, wrought iron chairs.

A neutral colour range
for sophistication

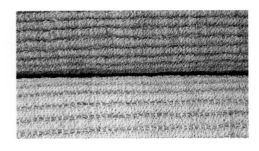

NATURAL MATTING
▲ Coir matting is a tough floor covering that looks especially good in a neutral interior.

This perfectly styled, contemporary dining room is a great example of style on a budget. It is an achievable look for a first-time home owner or someone constantly moving house and wanting to keep furnishings to an absolute minimum.

The room is decorated using off-white emulsion paint, with the addition of one wall that has had a soft mushroom stripe applied, also with emulsion paint. This is a very cost-effective form of decorating; just use a plumb line or ruler and masking tape to achieve the stripes.

The carpet is a fine check in soft caramel and cream, as is the top tablecloth, and the change of scale between the two patterns means they do not compete. They are also broken up by the undercloth with its flowing calligraphy motif. By using floor-length tablecloths, you can employ any old table; it could even be an old metal patio table, or a tabletop made of chipboard.

FINE FURNITURE
▶ Natural timber will always enhance a contemporary neutral colour scheme as it is full of tone and texture.

Texture is as important as pattern in a room like this, and this design supplies lots of it in a very complementary way. The softness of the carpet, the coldness of smooth wrought iron, the rustic aged timber, cane basket work and the distressed terracotta work together

well. You will find that textures derived from nature always work successfully in this type of scheme.

As this is a neutrally coloured room, it relies on changes of tone to be successful. Look at it as if it were a black and white photograph and you will see ample variation. The scheme is lifted by the introduction of a colour accent in the form of two green plants. Another advantage to this colour scheme is that it looks just as effective in the evening with its complementary candlelight from the chandelier hanging above the table.

ADDING TEXTURE

Texture is as important as pattern in a neutral colour scheme. The carpet featured above could have been replaced with the natural coir matting shown opposite for a slightly varied effect.

Colours of the
Italian renaissance

This traditional dining room is the perfect location for a formal dinner party. The terracotta red walls offer warmth during the day, but take on a far softer appearance in the evening. This colour works particularly well in candlelight, and as the dining room is the one room in the house that you are most likely to light in this manner, it is the perfect colour (together with darker and lighter tones) to use here.

The fully upholstered dining chairs are covered in sky blue damask that contrasts strongly with the terracotta walls. The chairs have been finished off with a rope detail at the back – don't forget that the backs of dining chairs are usually seen more than the front. Although the wall panelling below the dado rail enhances the formal air of this room, the lack of heavily dressed curtains adds a simplicity to it that ensures the overall effect is not too grand.

The room is lit by a large central pendant in a rococo style which is very masculine in appearance with strong lines. A dining room lit by one central light will always benefit from having a dimmer switch fitted so that the levels of lighting can be varied very simply to alter the atmosphere within the room.

There is nothing nicer than a fully dressed dining table. The china and table dressings have just as

SMALL DETAILS
Choose your cutlery and china to enhance the colours of your finished room. Here the deep red rim is the perfect match for the painted walls.

SETTING THE STYLE
◀ Damask fabric and rich historical colours have been combined with carefully chosen accessories to create this elegant and stylish dining room.

profile tradition and class

CAREFUL CONTRASTS

▼ Contrasting colours just a few tones removed from their primary shades of red and blue are used to great effect in this traditional room.

much of an impact on the finished look of your room as do the upholstery and curtaining. Choose cutlery and china that is sympathetic to the decor of your room, not only in terms of colour but also in shape and pattern; they should all enhance your chosen theme.

Aquamarine and white
for casual dining

Casual dining has now become more popular than ever, with many houses substituting the traditional dining room for an eating area within one of the other rooms in the house. This could be a corner of the living room or, as in this case, an area off the kitchen.

This particular kitchen and dining area has been housed in a

HARMONY IN THE HOME

This combined kitchen and dining room is home to a traditional solid fuel cooker, yet it retains a very modern feel. The aquamarine and white are a striking and fresh combination working together harmoniously because they are both such cool colours.

ADDING INTEREST

A variety of glassware adds interest to the dining area without altering the colour scheme or overpowering the rest of the decor.

CHOOSING THE ACCENT

An accent colour, in this case deep lilac, always adds life to a room made up of almost equal proportions of two colours. The lilac works so well because while it is taken from the same side of the colour wheel as the aquamarine, making it an harmonious shade, it is also almost opposite the aquamarine so contrasts strongly.

new conservatory. The main structure has been painted aquamarine, a refreshing change from white, and has been taken as the basis for a cool colour scheme. The modern etched glass table, for example, brings aquamarine into the dining space, and the chairs introduce chrome. This theme of glass and chrome has been continued on the table, with its glass plates and accessories.

The colour used in the kitchen area is warm and light. The unit doors and dresser top are manufactured from limed oak while the carcasses and surrounding walls are painted a simple ivory. A black solid fuel cooker takes centre stage, and although it is a traditional design, the whole area retains a contemporary feel because of the chrome fittings and kitchenware.

This room is so successful because of the colour flow between the two areas. There is a distinct division but the colours continue without jarring. The soft caramel of the kitchen units, for example, is introduced to the dining area via the seagrass flooring, and the black of the ceramic floor is echoed in the table legs and cutlery.

The finished area is enhanced by the introduction of an accent colour. The deep lilac napkins, flowers and teacloth add relief to the aquamarine and caramel colour scheme.

Bedrooms

The bedroom is the one room in the house where you can truly shut out the world. It is also the most personal place in the home, and the decor should reflect this.

There are no hard-and-fast rules when decorating a bedroom, yet the finished space should be relaxing and comfortable, offer a suitable place to sleep and, if the room is to be multi-functional, then a desk or table at which to work should be included.

Choose colours carefully as they need to look as good in the evening as in the morning light. It is best to avoid very bright hues as they may prove disturbing if the room is used during a bout of illness. However, should you want a bolder colour scheme, the earthy and toning shades of terracotta, rich cream and black can offer an effective option.

PEACE AND QUIET
◀ Crisp, calming blue and white creates a timeless and relaxing colour scheme for a bedroom.

MIXING PRIMARY COLOURS

▶ The primary colours of blue and yellow are the base colours for this contemporary scheme. All the other, secondary, colours are derived from them. The result is harmonious, yet fun.

SUBTLE SHADES

▼ Muted shades of aquamarine and cream are mixed with natural and colourwashed timber to create this restful bedroom.

Reds and burgundies
bring Eastern

If you are looking for a warm bedroom that has a traditional feel combined with just a touch of glamour, then a bedroom with a hint of Eastern promise could be the perfect solution.

Searching for a decorative theme, such as this, can be enormous fun and by looking through books and magazines you will quickly glean all sorts of ideas. The essence of this type of room is not purely limited to the decor, however. The numerous artifacts – all based on the same theme – may at first appear to be small touches but they make all the difference to recreating that certain overall ambience.

FANTASY FABRICS

▼ The silk wall hanging enhances the already exotic atmosphere of this romantic bedroom. The neutral tones on the walls behind the bed make it even more of a focal point.

The warm tones of burnt orange and rich reds are an important element in this particular look. Glorious silks, heavy cottons and beaded and embroidered fabrics add a richness and opulence that is inherent in any Eastern scheme. Beautifully carved pieces of furniture in mid- to dark tones can be chosen to provide the most elaborate of beds and storage cupboards.

The room featured opposite has a kelim rug on the floor, and the bed is dressed in antique white lace together with an array of gold-spotted silk cushions. The ornate and exotic lamp is evocative of warm Eastern nights, and the bowl of fruit reminds us of the tastes of the Orient.

The way in which many different patterns can be used successfully in one room is illustrated particularly well here. The plain

promise

background on the walls and floor and simple bedding give breathing space and the deep earth shades featured in the patterned fabrics mean that they meld together well. The white bedcover provides contrast and relief as well as providing a focal point.

COMBINING PATTERNS

▲ Rugs and Oriental artifacts are important elements in the Eastern influenced room. Although there are many different patterns here, they work well together as the colours are limited to shades of the same four – deep red, gold, blue and sage green.

DARK AND LIGHT

◀ Warm reds, burnt orange, and gold are teamed with an elephant motif on this canopied bed. The white sheet and pillowcases throw the richer colours into vivid relief and also retain a sense of coolness and freshness.

Cheerful yellows
make for summer

This sunny bedroom is warm and relaxing, and it has been deco-rated to illustrate perfectly the use of colour as a backdrop (see pages 20-1). The main feature in the room is the fabric drape behind the bedstead, drawing attention to the bed itself. By dec-orating the walls and floors simply and without pattern, the backdrop is enhanced as there is nothing to draw the eye away from its attractive leafy design.

The colour scheme of the room has been chosen to enhance this fabric, ensuring the shades of green in the design are

A FRESH AWAKENING
This sunny bedroom, uses both pattern and tone to create a stylishly simple room with plenty of visual interest.

sunshine

TONAL VARIATIONS
By using elements of varying tones of one colour these elements will enhance each other. Because green is derived from mixing yellow with blue it is a natural companion for yellow.

prominent. The different tones and shades of yellow both in plain paints and the various patterns bring depth and visual interest to this mainly monochromatic colour scheme. The yellow pattern fabrics have been chosen because they are a mixture of stripes, checks and compact flowing designs which all work well together. To balance the green in the fabric, greenery has been introduced on the dressing table.

The choice of furniture retains the light and fresh feel of the room. The openness of the tables make the areas on either side of the bed and below the window as spacious as possible.

The curtains have a plain band running down the leading edges to add detail to their design, and the heading – tabs that are tied over the curtain pole – has been chosen to keep the overall effect simple yet stylish. The curtains fall slightly on the floor, creating a softness to counteract the hard lines that can sometimes appear when a curtain meets the line of the floor.

Compare this room with the living room featured on pages 28-9. Green and yellow have been used for both rooms but in

SUMMERTIME IN PROVENCE
This provençal fabric would give the same warmth to a room, but a totally different look as the patterns are so much more detailed. The end result would not be light as, say, in the room opposite.

different proportions. Both rooms are very successfully decorated, but try to imagine them painted in reverse and the effect is not nearly as attractive. Yellows are so right for bedrooms – sunny and relaxing. Somehow greens speak too much of the great outdoors.

Clever contrasts in
deep plum

Although they are not the most overly used of colours, plum and green work particularly well together in this bedroom. They tone together well because they are fairly close to each other on the colour wheel. The patchwork quilt was the starting point for the decor, and the plum and green featured in one of the fabrics were chosen to decorate the room.

A striped wallpaper combining both colours adds detail to the wall. It is contained within two borders of soft plum on the skirting and picture rail. Similarly, the bedding is a combination of two colours, plum and cream, both of which feature in the quilt. Green has also been introduced via a leaf border on the cream pillows. By using cream pillows instead of green, the bed doesn't look heavy and dull because the cream adds a strong contrast to the plum and a freshness to the overall scheme.

Getting the right colour for bedding can prove a problem. I now dye my own bed linen to match any colour scheme I have a problem with. Machine dyes are very simple to use, and have good results. Fabric paints also mean you can decorate sheets and pillowcases using stencils and stamps, so there is no excuse for using plain bedding, unless you prefer it.

PULLING IT ALL TOGETHER

▶ The patchwork quilt, wallpaper and wrought-iron bed give the room its traditional feel. This is further enhanced by the picture rail and sash window and the whole has been unified by drawing predominantly upon the harmonious colours of green and plum for the decor.

PERSONALIZING YOUR BEDDING

◀ The introduction of stencilled or stamped motifs on fabrics means the designer is limited only by his or her imagination. It is the perfect way to introduce harmonious or contrasting colours to a room.

and green

The curtains add height to the room because they are just left to hang without tiebacks. By using floor-length curtains in this way you form two vertical, strong lines of colour that draw the eye line vertically up the wall to the pelmet. To enhance this still further, a striped fabric could be used or a contrasting strip of fabric along each leading edge of the curtains.

As a spot of accent colour, the dressing table is painted a deep, but faded blue, a colour once again taken from the quilt where it is found in very small quantities.

IMPROVING PROPORTION
▲ Striped wallpapers add height to a room whose walls have been divided by a picture rail.

Bathrooms

Bathrooms, like kitchens, are expensive, so it is very important to get the layout correct. Once you have decided on the best plan for the room, you can turn your attention to choosing a theme or style in which to decorate it. There is now an ever increasing number of decorative products available, everything from ceramic tiles to solid vinyl wall coverings and mildew resistant paints, giving an unlimited choice when decorating a bathroom.

A bathroom can be classically chic, using granite and marble, or bright and sunny, a room to lift your spirits, even on the coldest of mornings. Either way, before purchasing even the smallest item, you must be sure of the finished look you wish to achieve.

Blues can be used to create a nautical theme, and there are many accessories available to enhance this look. Or you may decorate your bathroom with plain white ceramics and a white suite, giving yourself the perfect basic scheme around which you can create numerous different schemes over the years.

A small bathroom can benefit from an artistic approach. Make the room appear much larger by enlisting the help of a trompe l'oeil mural. Or transform your small, dark room into a Grecian palace or Victorian theatre with heavy velvet drapes drawn back above your bath, giving you a front row seat. Don't forget about any architectural details you may have; exploit whatever you have to hand. When you think about it, decorating a bathroom can be as serious or as much fun as you like.

SETTING OFF THE SUITE
Yellow walls and brown tongue and groove blend harmoniously and make the bathroom suite crisp in its whiteness.

BLUE FOR YOU

▶ A traditional wooden clad bathroom can be given a new lease of life with the addition of colour. The bright yellow tulips with the mass of green leaves is the perfect accent for a blue room – blue and yellow make green. Colour mixing at its best.

FRESHEN UP

▼ An existing decorative coving and feature fireplace set the scene for this white bathroom suite. A green colour-wash and accessories, gives the room a classi-cally cool atmosphere because green comes from the cool side of the colour wheel.

Cool pastels compose
a tranquil

Ceramic tiles offer one of the most versatile wall finishes for the bathroom, yet this room proves paint can be equally as versatile. The roughly plastered walls have been given a covering of a soft cream paint, and this has created the base for a colourwash effect for the lower two thirds of the wall. The height chosen for splitting the colour is very important. The wall is usually divided one third up its total height, but in warmer climes the colour is usually taken higher up, as in this bathroom. The colourwash effect adds texture to the room, and contrasts well with the cool smoothness of the ceramic sanitary wear.

Ceramic tiles in a blue design sympathetic to the colourwash have been used to full height in the shower area. In such areas, you should be careful that the chosen wall covering is suitable for a space where water is constantly running on its surface: ceramics are the perfect solution.

White muslin has been used as a feature in the room, softly contrasting with the cream of the walls. Many people are worried about combining a white bathroom suite with cream walls, but as long as the white is echoed elsewhere in the room, it will work. Many Victorian style bathroom suites are teamed with cream and black ceramic tiles. All that is normally needed is the addition of white towels or a wallpaper combining

KEEPING IT FRESH
▶ Rough plastered walls and a colourwash paint finish is teamed with white muslin and Grecian style accessories in this pastel bathroom.

TEXTURAL CONTRASTS
◀ Mixing textures can have as much of an effect in a room as the mixing of patterns.

backdrop

THE SMALLER THINGS

⚠ Choosing the right accessories is very important – look for complementary colours and stylish containers to fit your decor.

white and cream in order to tie together the whole scheme. Remember, too, that a white suite will always look crisper when teamed with cream, and the cream richer.

The exposed floorboards have been stained in a checkerboard design, adding further texture and interest to the room. The purple squares are a deeper tone than the grey colourwash, adding tonal interest. Grecian style accessories complete the picture in this stylish bathroom.

Lemon, mint and orange —
citrus colours for a

This family bathroom has all the accessories you would normally find in a nautically themed room: the fish mirror, the boats, and the wooden fish swimming around the window. The nice thing about this room, however, is the addition of colour; bright, spirit-lifting, citrus colours.

The bath and vanity basin are of a traditional 1930s' design, and the large black and white tiles are reminiscent of the same period. But with the introduction of the orange dado moulded tiles, lemon walls and a spearmint bath panel and window frame, the room has taken on a very contemporary feel. Such

AN INVIGORATING BATHROOM
This family bathroom would lift your spirits on the dullest of days. The bright yellow and mint green work so well together, particularly as they are off-set by the orange accents.

bright bathroom

CHOOSING YOUR SHADES

▶ Citrus colours bring summer warmth to a small, dark room.

A SPLASH OF COLOUR

▶ Ceramic tiles are the perfect tool for introducing – or reinforcing – the colour and pattern in even the smallest of bathrooms.

citrus shades work well together as they are so closely related and they certainly add a zing to the bathroom. As most of the colour has been injected by a quick lick of a paintbrush, when fashions change or boredom sets in, the bathroom can just as quickly be transformed once again.

You could transform an existing 1930s' style bathroom with its black and white tiles and black ceramic mouldings in a similar way. If you didn't want to replace the black mouldings you could paint them with a ceramic paint. You would get a similar effect, but unfortunately it will not be as durable as it is only ceramic paints that can be fired that last well.

One of the benefits of using ceramic tiles in a room like this is the variety of colours now available, so you can inject any colour over any size patch that you desire. Of course, there are many patterned tiles, too, and by mixing them with plain tiles, an infinite number of designs can be created. Some of the very shiny tiles are produced using a majolica glaze, which gives great depth of colour and, over time, small cracks appear in the glaze, adding an aged look to the tile. Look around for small mosaic tiles and create your own designs to either cover part of a wall or make as decorative inserts.

Hallways

First impressions are very important, and the first glimpse that many people have of your home is quite often the hall. It does not matter how hard you have planned and beautifully decorated your other rooms, if the linking areas leave a lot to be desired, the effect is never quite the same.

Because of the amount of traffic through a hallway, the decorative elements should be durable. Likewise, try to ensure you have the maximum amount of light. If this is at a minimum, consider opening up doorways into rooms that have natural light available. Artificial lighting lacks character, so highlight areas of interest, such as bookshelves, the stairwell, or a seating area.

Hallways, by their very nature, normally contain many interesting angles and shapes, so use these to your advantage to create an interesting space within your home.

GRAND ILLUSIONS

▼ Narrow hallways should be decorated with caution. The white here maximizes the illusion of space and the warm colours in the painting on the far wall make the hall appear shorter as the wall advances rather than recedes. Position pictures on one wall only or the room will appear even narrower.

SETTING THE SCENE

▼ A blue colourwash on the areas of paintwork both upstairs and down, link this old, yet amazingly contemporary hallway. The contrast is provided by the red stair carpet and flowers.

LIGHTING UP

◄ Lighting should be used to highlight areas within the hallway, such as the stairwell featured here. All too often they can appear dark and claustrophobic.

Cool colours –
a warm welcome

This smart hall ensures that the flow from one room to another is as interesting as possible. To achieve this, the colours have been selected from adjacent rooms and cleverly combined in this communal area.

The wall has been split using a dado rail below which is panelled with a traditional moulding. To provide extra detail, an additional cut-out, Gothic-style strip has been attached to the dado moulding. This is a nice contrast to the hard lines of the other mouldings.

The heavier of the two greens featured in the hall has been used to pick out areas below the dado, enhancing its decorative details. To keep the hall looking as spacious as possible, a fresh blue-green from the cool side of the colour wheel has been painted on the upper wall area.

Paint is a practical and versatile finish, ideal for areas of heavy usage. Likewise, the flooring is a hard-wearing checkerboard design of black and white tiles that enhances the traditional feel of the hall. The checkered floor continues into the kitchen which helps to enlarge the hallway because the eye is led into another space. The kitchen cupboard doors, painted to match the hallway walls, also increase the feeling of space by uniting the two areas still further.

SPACE ENHANCING
▶ Decorative mouldings and the planned use of colour creates a fresh and effective hallway. The palest shades of green make the space appear larger than it really is, as does the sweep of the checkerboard floor that leads the eye into the kitchen and other rooms.

MAKING THE MOST OF IT
◀ Cool colours have the ability to open up the smallest of spaces as they make rooms look larger. Team them with cream for a soft effect.

Neutrals and checks
for that country feel

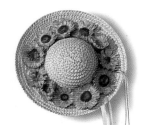

DRIED FLOWERS
▲ Country accessories are very important to the finished look of a hallway. Flower arrangements like these would make a perfect accent for, say, a blue or green hallway.

MIXING PATTERNS
▶ Red and orange are warm colours that introduce a welcoming and cosy feel to a room. Different patterns can work well together as long as they are based on the same colours.

This country hall has also been decorated using paint. It may have this in common with the hall featured on the previous page, but due to the type of colours chosen, the look really is quite dramatically different.

Here, the colours are taken from the warm side of the colour wheel creating the perfect atmosphere for the entrance to a house. As this is an area with plenty of headroom and open spaces, these colours are the perfect option as they visually draw in the walls and ceiling, making a room look more inviting.

A natural floor matting has been used to add a mellow texture to the floor and it continues up the staircase. The mahogany turned hand rail and spindles contrast well with both the walls and floor, toning in with the chosen colour scheme. This wood finish is also echoed in both the curtain pole and the wall-mounted clock positioned half-way up the stairs. The area under the stairs has been painted to blend with the walls.

To create a certain style you need to enlist the help of some elements that have a particularly evocative feel and enormous fun can be had searching out the perfect accessories. Here, an informal element has been added through the ultimate in country fabric design, the red and white check fabrics.

MAKING AN ENTRANCE
Check fabrics in traditional colours are always successful in a setting like this one as the colours are bold but the pattern not too overwhelming.

These particular curtains sweep onto the floor which is especially practical when hanging over a front or back door as it helps to keep draughts at bay.

The pieces of occasional furniture and accessories have a rustic appearance and work well in the finished room as they offset the red, contrasting accent colour. The chair by the hall table has been incorporated into its setting by adding a cushion made of red and white checks, but this time a small gingham fabric has been used rather than the larger squares of the curtains. The scale is just perfect.

Mustard, saffron and mace:
spice colours

SOFT AND FLOWING
The use of warm neutrals and carefully chosen fabrics ensures a light, classically styled stairway.

Neutrals are always easy to live with, and the warmer tones especially so. This wonderfully classical hallway is simple in its styling. The arched windows are a major feature and the chosen curtain style accentuates their shape. The use of sheers allows for maximum light to flood into the house and the knotted and draped swags add a little colour and interest. Never attempt to hang straight topped curtains on arched windows as they won't hang correctly and the finished look will be messy. For the best

for warmth and softness

and neatest end result, curtains for windows like this should be carefully cut out around a template of the arch from which they are to hang.

The caramel coloured carpet is a deep enough tone to be practical without appearing heavy. The walls are also decorated in a neutral shade and with a soft sandstone blockwork effect. This can be achieved by either using a paint finish or by hanging a faux effect wallpaper of the same design.

To add tonal variety to the room, the wooden staircase and window frame have been painted in a matt white. This also makes the walls and carpet appear richer. The top of the newel post has been marbled to add subtle interest.

Once again it is the accessories that enhance the feel of the finished room by providing deeper, richer tones within the neutral colour scheme. The terracotta urns, small busts and bowls have been grouped together to add depth and considerable style to the windowsill. In addition, the golden velvet and brocade cushions at the other end of the sill are positioned to create a seating area from which to view the outside world. Decorative items like these always have a stronger effect on a room when grouped together. If the terracotta items has been spaced along the window, for example, they would have lost their impact.

A LITTLE SOMETHING
▲ Natural cotton and jute accessories look good in either a classical or contemporary setting. Their neutral tones don't jar and their texture is endlessly satisfying.

GENTLY DOES IT
▼ Spicy and natural colours – especially when combined in subtly patterned wallpapers like the marble-effect one here – work very well with plain sheer fabrics, as the subtle colours don't overwhelm the fine quality.

Children's rooms

Whether you are decorating a school-aged child's bedroom or a nursery, you must always put safety first. Ensure that all key pieces of furniture pass safety regulations, and that any paints you use are lead free. Paint is the perfect choice when decorating a child's bedroom and any artistic outbursts with a felt-tipped pen can soon be put right. Paint is also washable, so sticky fingers are not a problem.

Now that you know the safety of your child has been considered, you can get down to the enjoyable task of styling the room. There is one element that must be added to a child's room that doesn't apply to any other in the house, and that is the colourful addition of toys and clothes. You have two basic choices: a busy, colourful scheme where the toys and clutter blend into the room, or a room with the simple use of colour where the toys add extra colour and tone, and become a feature in their own right. The rooms illustrated on these pages and overleaf on pages 74-7 show you examples of both styles. When planning the decor, also remember that unless they have the benefit of a separate playroom, most children will have many toys, clothes and books to be stored, so careful consideration must be made when planning the room.

HAPPY DAYS

▼ In years to come, this sunny nursery could be transformed by the addition of a single bed with a colourful bed cover and matching new border, perhaps featuring some tonal contrasts – perfect for a growing child.

GETTING THE BALANCE RIGHT

▶ The colours in this room are bright enough and the design stylized enough for any age of child. Two such contrasting colours could look quite different by making one of them predominate.

BUSY TIMES

▼ This restful blue is the perfect background for any amount of colourful clutter.

A feminine bedroom in
ice cream pink

This soft strawberry and cream room acts as the perfect backdrop for a colourful bed cover and toys. The walls have been divided with a dado rail which is decorated below with cream and pink stripes of paint. The decor is simple and a balance is achieved when the paint colour used above the dado is introduced below, via the painted cupboard and storage chest. This is further enhanced by the colours below

FIT FOR A PRINCESS
▼ This simply decorated little girl's bedroom is the perfect setting for a night of sweet dreams. Pink and cream makes for a very peaceful combination.

being taken above the dado in the form of little bows, the bed drape and also on the mounts around the pictures.

The pictures were made by painting or stamping simple motifs onto white card using the deepest colour from the decor. They were then framed and grouped on the wall and successfully enhance the simplicity of the colour scheme. The crown motif has also been enlarged, cut from timber and painted the same colour as the dado rail to create a novel corona for the bed. It has been completed by the simple sheer drapes falling down to floor level on each side of the bed. The bright quilt cover has been made simply using large appliqué shapes and, if you so desired, you could repeat the motifs used in the pictures on the wall and in suitable toning colours.

A low playing or working area has been created by the small folding table and two children's wicker chairs that have been painted to blend into the scheme. Such miniature furniture is widely available, is easy to paint and is the perfect way to bring a child's eye view into a room. In a room like this, the brightly coloured toys provide all the colour accents you could possibly need.

FEMININE SHADES
◀ Pretty pinks create a softly-coloured bedroom. The touches of green give a lift to what might otherwise be too much pink.

ADDING A LITTLE SOMETHING
▲ Simple motifs like these teddy bears can be introduced to add interest to a bedroom and they can be painted or stamped in any colour to complement your colour scheme.

Paintbox colours
spell fun for a

Bright colours and a mixture of pattern all fire a child's imagination and creativity, and the bedroom featured here is the perfect example of achieving this without giving the illusion of chaos. The colours used are bright but harmonious, because they are related. The main colour – green – is derived from yellow which is the other predominantly used colour.

There is plenty of interest in this room. For example, a spotted wallpaper has been used above the picture rail. This is a good alternative to using it on the main wall as it would have been too busy there, and the plain white wall acts as a better background to the curtains and bedding.

The carpet is green, and the same colour is also used for a spotted bed valance, a practical option when you consider dusty shoes rubbing against the bed. To maintain the green theme, the curtains are bound with a white and green check framing the larger green plaid, and the heading is a simple design of ties that are inserted between the main fabric and lining.

The contrasting colour of canary yellow has been used on the woodwork, most noticeably on the chest that provides much needed storage in a child's room. The same yellow has also been used on the handy peg rail from which useful, patterned green and yellow drawstring storage bags hang.

ANIMAL MAGIC
▶ This creative child's bedroom would raise the spirits on the dullest of days. The riot of patterns are held together by using mainly yellow and green and an animal theme.

DOTTING ABOUT
◀ Dots are great fun in a child's room and can be added to just about anything and in any colour – toning or contrasting, depending on the effect you want to achieve.

child's room

The quilt cover introduces other colours into the room, and the stylized farm yard animals add a motif theme. While the spots and checks are bright and fun, animals such as these add substance to the room. The young occupant is displaying his or her version of the farmyard animals featured in the fabric.

STORING IT UP
▲ Drawstring bags in coordinating fabrics offer an effective storage solution and can be valuable colour accents.

STOCKISTS AND CONTRIBUTORS LIST

UNITED KINGDOM

CONTRIBUTORS

Artisan
Trade Showroom
4a Union Court
20-22 Union Road
London SW4 6JP
Tel: 0171 498 6974
Fax: 0171 498 2989
(Contemporary and classic
curtain rails)

Colefax & Fowler
Tel: 0181 874 6484
(for stockists)

Cope & Timmins Ltd
Head Office
Angel Road Works
Angel Road
Edmonton
London N18 3AY
with branches in Birmingham,
Bristol, Glasgow,
Leeds and Manchester
(window furnishings)

Crown Paints
Tel: 01254 704951
(for stockists)

Crowson
Headquarters
Crowson House
Bellbrook Park
Uckfield
East Sussex TN22 1QZ
Tel: 01825 761044
(furniture, furnishings and
made-to-measure service)

Crucial Trading Ltd
The Market Hall
Craven Arms
Shropshire SY7 9NY
Tel: 01588 673666
(Natural floor coverings)

Descamps
Corner Descamps
at Liberty
Regent Street
London W1R 6AH
Tel: 0171 734 1234 (Ext 2270)
(Bedroom and bathroom linen,
towels and dressing gowns)

The Design Archives
Tel: 01202 753248

Designers Guild
267/271 & 277
Kings Road
London SW3 5EN

Dulux Paints
Tel: 01753 550555
(customer services)

Fired Earth
Twyford Mill
Oxford Road
Adderbury
Oxon OX17 3HP
Tel: 01295 812088
(Tiles, flooring, fabrics)

**The General Trading
Company**
144 Sloane Street
London SW1X 9BL
Tel: 0171 730 0411

Graham & Greene
4,7 & 10 Elgin Crescent
London W11 2JA
Tel: 0171 727 4594
Fax: 0171 729 9717
and
164 Regents Park Road
London NW1 8XN
Tel: 0171 586 2960
Fax: 0171 483 0901
(Lifestyle shop featuring vast
selection of products from UK
and around the world, including
rugs, fabrics, lighting, furniture
and decorative accessories.)

Habitat
Branches throughout UK
Tel: 0171 255 2545

Heal's
196 Tottenham Court Road
London W1P 9LD
Tel: 0171 636 1666

Laura Ashley
Tel: 01686 622116
(customer services)

MacCulloch & Wallis Ltd
25 Dering Street
London W1R 0BH
Tel: 0171 629 0311
(fabrics with extensive range of
silks)

Nimbus
Delbanco Meyer & Company
Portland House
Ryland ROad
London NW3 3EB
Tel: 0171 468 3000
(cotton and linen bedroom
accessories)

Osborne & Little
Tel: 0181 675 2255
(for stockists)

The Pier (Retail) Ltd
Head Office
153 Milton Park
Abingdon
OX14 4SD
Tel: 01235 821088

Prêt à Vivre
39-41 Lonsdale Road
Queens Park
London NW6 6RA
Tel: 0171 328 4500
Fax: 0171 328 4515
(curtains, blinds, fabrics)

Pukka Palace
174 Tower Bridge Road
London SE1
Tel: 0171 234 0000
Fax: 0171 234 0110
(Natural fabrics)

Sanderson
Tel: 0181 440 1397
(for enquiries)

Texas Homecare
Homecharm House
Parkfarm
Wellingborough
Northampton
Tel: 01933 679679
(branches throughout the UK)

Viners of Sheffield plc
Viners House
106 Brent Terrace
London NW2 1BZ
Tel: 0181 450 8900

AUSTRALIA

BBC Hardware
Branches throughout Australia
Contact Head Office
Building A, Cnr Cambridge &
Chester Streets
Epping NSN 2121
Tel: 02 876 0888

HomeHardware
17 branches, contact:
65 Ashmore Road
Alexandria NSW 2015
New South Wales
Tel: 519 9066

Mitre 10
35 branches, contact:
Access Via 12 Dansu Court
Hallam
Princess Highway Victoria 3803
Victoria
Tel: 796 4999

True Value Hardware
15 branches, contact
136 7 Main North Road
Para West Hills SA 5096
South Australia
Tel: 281 2244

True Value Hardware
56 Branches, contact
16 Cambridge Street
Rocklea Queensland 4106
Queensland
Tel: 892 0892

Makit Hardware
35 branches, contact
Kimmer Place
Queens Park WA 6107
Tel: 351 8001

NEW ZEALAND

Carpet Court
57 Barrys Point Road
Takapuna
Tel: 09 489 9094

Levene & Co Ltd
Head Office
Harris Road
East Tamaki
Tel: 09 274 4211

Mitre 10
169 Wairu Road
Glenfield
Tel: 09 443 9900

Placemakers
Support Office
150 Marua Road
Panmure
Tel: 09 535 5100

Resene Colour Shops
14 Link Drive
Glenfield
Tel: 09 444 4387

Acknowledgements

The author and publishers would like to thank the following companies and their PR agencies for the loan of photographs and props used in this book.
Artisan Curtain Rails: 41t
Cope & Timmins Ltd: 29t, 71t
Crown Paints: 5
Crowson Fabrics Furnishings Wallcoverings: 23, 52/53t
Crucial Trading Ltd: 44t, 48
Dorma: 51b
Dulux: cover, 8, 11, 16, 39, 45, 59, 61b, 69, 74
Fired Earth: 63b
Habitat: 38b, 44b
Laura Ashley: title
Nimbus: 25tr
Magnet: 35t
The Pier: 59t, 61t
Pret a Vivre: 38t, 55b
Primavera: 23
Sanderson Collection: 15
Viners of Sheffield plc: 46t

Picture credits
Abode: 25tl, 65t, 73t
Elizabeth Whiting Associates: cover detail, 27, 29, 33, 36, 42, 47, 50, 51t,58b, 64b
Lizzie Orme: Contents left, 6/7, 43b
Paul Ryan/International Interiors: (Frances Halliday) 25bl; (Jo Nahem) 25br; (John Fell Clark) 34; (Rob Brandt) 40; (Frances Halliday) 62; (Rex Jackson) 70
Rupert Horrox: 16, 53b (Graham & Greene)
Dominic Blackmore/Homes & Ideas/Robert Harding Syndication: Contents right, 21
Options/IPC Magazines/Robert Harding Syndication: 24b
Polly Wreford/Homes & Gardens/Robert Harding Syndication: 26
Brian Harrison/Homes & Gardens/Robert Harding Syndication: 35
Lucinda Symons/Ideal Home/Robert Harding Syndication: 43t
Dominc Blackmore/Ideal Home/Robert Harding Syndication: 54
Lucinda Symons/Ideal Home/Robert Harding Syndication: 57
Andreas von Einsiedel/Homes & Gardens/Robert Harding Syndication: 65
Trevor Richards/Homes & Gardens/Robert Harding Syndication: 67
Dominic Blackmore/Homes & Ideas/Robert Harding Syndication: 73b
James Merrell/Homes & Gardens/Robert Harding Syndication: 77

Index